THE BELL KEEPER

*The story of Sophia
and the massacre of the Indians
at Gnadenhutten, Ohio, in 1782*

Marilyn Seguin

BRANDEN PUBLISHING COMPANY
Boston

Library of Congress Cataloguing-in-Publication Data

Seguin, Marilyn.
  The bell keeper : the story of Sophia and the massacre of the
Indians at Gnadenhutten, Ohio, in 1782 / Marilyn W. Seguin.
      p. cm.
  Includes bibliographical references.
  ISBN 0-8283-2009-8 (trade paper : acid-free paper)
  1. Gnadenhutten Massacre, Gnadenhutten, Ohio, 1782--
Juvenile literature.
  2. Moravian Indians--History--18th century--Juvenile literature.
  3. Moravian Indians--Missions--Ohio--Gnadenhutten--
Juvenile literature.
  4. Moravian Church--Missions--Ohio--Gnadenhutten--
Juvenile literature.
  5. Indians of North America--History--Revolution, 1775-1783--
Juvenile literature.
  6. Indians of North America--Wars--1775-1783--
Juvenile literature.
  [1. Gnadenhutten Massacre, Gnadenhutten, Ohio, 1782. 2.
Moravian Indians--History--18th century.   3. Indians of North
America--History--Revolution, 1775-1783.]   I. Title.
E99.M9S44 1995
973.3'37--dc20   95-9996
                                                         CIP
                                                          AC

BRANDEN PUBLISHING COMPANY
17 Station Street
Box 843 Brookline Village
Boston, MA 02147

For bells are the voice of the church;
They have tones that touch and search
The hearts of young and old.

—————Longfellow, *The Bells of San Blas*

Dedication

This book is dedicated with love to my mother, Deanie Weymouth.

Acknowledgments

I first read about Sophia and her family in a fascinating book, *Blackcoats Among the Delaware*, an account of the life and work of David Zeisberger written by Earl Olmstead (Kent State University Press, 1991). After finishing Olmstead's book, I drove the sixty miles from my home to Goshen to visit Sophia's grave site. It was then that I decided to write *The Bell Keeper*.

I am indebted to many people who helped with the research, writing and illustrating of this book. Specifically, I thank my husband Rollie and my children Scott and Katy for their encouragement and careful reading of early versions of the manuscript. Thanks also to my friend, writer and photographer Jane Ann Turzillo, whose photos appear throughout the book. A special thanks to artist and teacher Judy Botz Newhall, whose beautiful painting appears on the cover.

I am grateful to Arthur W. McGraw for permission to reproduce here three pages of the clarified image of Zeisberger's Speller; and to Barb McKeown, Manager of the Gnadenhutten Historical Site, for permission to include photos of the reconstructed buildings and the monuments. The map of Ohio and the surrounding area was designed by Karen Andrews, under the direction of Dr. Howard Veregin of the Department of Geography at Kent State University.

Once again, thanks to Edi Morrill for keyboarding another manuscript at the last minute. Finally, I'd like to thank my friend Nancy Jensen for hounding me to finish writing this book--and to get started on the next one.

Prologue

G nadenhutten (Tents of Grace) was a pretty town built upon the banks of the peaceful Muskingum River in Ohio Country. The villagers were mostly Indians, converted to Christianity by the Moravian missionaries, whose beliefs included complete pacifism--even in the brewing conflict of the American Revolution.

Young Sophia led a quiet and happy life in Gnadenhutten, until the summer of 1781, when suddenly she found herself and her family caught up in the fierce struggle between the American Long Knives and the British. What happened at Gnadenhutten in the spring of 1782 has been called one of the most atrocious crimes ever committed upon the Indians. Sophia was one of the few survivors.

In the face of grief, hunger, cold, and the loss of all she holds dear, Sophia sustained her faith and belief in the essential goodness of life. This is the story of her courage.

The Tuscarawas River (known to Sophia as the Muskingum River), as it flows near Gnadenhutten. Photo by Jane Turzillo.

Chapter 1

Sophia and Thomas stood on the river bank, skipping smooth, flat stones across the slow-moving water of the Muskingum River.

"Six, seven, eight!" Sophia shouted, counting the skips as her stone skimmed the surface. "I win! That's the most skips all day," she said, and slapped Thomas hard on the back.

"Pride goeth before a fall," said Thomas, and gave his friend a playful shove. Sophia landed on her behind on the soft moss that lined the river bank. "Besides, you don't win yet, Sophie," he said. "I have one more stone still." And Thomas threw his stone at the shiny surface of the water. The stone skipped once, twice, three times, and sank.

Thomas looked at his friend and grinned. "I never could beat you at skipping stones, Sophie. What's your secret?" Sophia started to tell him that it was the weight of the stone, not the shape, that made it a good skipper, when suddenly Thomas grabbed her arm and pulled her into the shadow of the forest. She squealed in protest, but Thomas put his hand roughly over her mouth, stopping her voice, and she tasted the mud of the river bank on his fingers. He dragged her into the shade of dense woods.

"Be quiet, Sophie," he whispered in her ear, still holding her tightly. "It's Chief Captain Pipe and his warriors, across the river. There," he said, removing his hand from her mouth and pointing down river. Sophia saw Chief Captain Pipe and a dozen braves decorated in war paint come out of the forest. The Indians led their horses to the river to drink.

Captain Pipe was the head chief of the Munsee Delaware tribe who lived far to the north of the Muskingum. Pipe and his people were firmly allied to the British who were fighting the Americans for possession of his land. Both Sophia and Thomas also knew that Pipe opposed the three Moravian Indian missionary settlements on the Muskingum River.

"Brother Zeisberger and Brother Edwards will not be pleased," whispered Sophia to her friend. "These Indians are painted for war, but they know we Indians at Gnadenhutten do not fight. To kill another is the greatest of sins. Why do they come back to our town after Brother Zeisberger sent them away?"

"Captain Pipe cares little for the words of Brother Zeisberger, Sophie. Pipe says we are Indians first and we owe allegiance to our red brothers and sisters, not to the God of the white man," said Thomas in her ear. But Sophia didn't understand his words. She had been born in Gnadenhutten, born into the Moravian Christian settlement her grandfather had helped build with the white Christian missionaries at the invitation of the great Delaware Chief Netawatwees.

The year before her birth, Netawatwees and his chiefs had proposed to the new Continental Congress that Ohio land become the 14th state and that it be governed by the Indians. Netawatwees then invited the Moravian missionaries and the converted Indian Brethren to move their missions from Pennsylvania to Ohio. Sophia's family had made the move, following their beloved leader, the missionary Brother David Zeisberger. Sophia had known no other home than Gnadenhutten, where she had lived all ten of her years with her parents, Josua and Sophia the Elder, and her sisters, Anna and Bathsheba.

Unlike Sophia, Thomas had not been born into a missionary settlement. Thomas' family had come to Gnadenhutten as converts only six years ago, when Thomas was eight. Thomas still talked about his former life and his old friends at the Delaware Indian village in which he had spent his early years. It was a life much different than what Sophia and Thomas knew at Gnadenhutten.

"We should hurry back to Gnadenhutten and tell the others that the warriors approach," said Sophia. Thomas nodded, and quietly the two children slipped into the forest and hurried back to their village.

When Thomas and Sophia reached Gnadenhutten, the streets were deserted. Most of the people were inside their cabins talking or reading, trying to stay out of the hot sun. It was a Sunday and no one was working in the community orchard or the family vegetable gardens, for Sunday was a day of rest for all the Brethren.

The village of Gnadenhutten consisted of nearly sixty wood cabins, arranged in neat rows. The cabins had pitched, shingled roofs that kept them snug and dry all year round. In spite of the August heat, thin wisps of smoke rose from the stone chimneys of a few of the cabins, and Sophia smelled the rich odors of food cooking. Her stomach growled with hunger, but there was not time to eat. Thomas and Sophia ran down the street toward the meeting house that also served as their church.

"We'll ring the church bell to warn our people," said Sophia, and she and Thomas raced toward the building.

At the end of the main street of Gnadenhutten stood the mission church and meeting house, a wooden structure big enough to hold everyone in the village-- men, women and children. On top of the roof, a small cupola sheltered the church bell from the weather. Sophia's own grandfather Joshua Sr., a skilled metal worker, had made the bell in Philadelphia. When Joshua Sr. and the others were invited to start a new mission town in Ohio, Joshua Sr. himself had carried the bell along the journey.

From the very beginning, the bell had each morning and evening summoned the villagers to worship, as well as to baptismals, to funerals, and to the special celebrations called Love Feasts held to celebrate every significant event that touched the lives of the Brethren at Gnadenhutten.

Sophia and Thomas scrambled through the unlocked door of the church. A heavy rope hung from the top of the bell into the room. Sophia reached the rope ahead of Thomas and she grasped it and pulled down on it hard. The bell rang clear and loud into the quiet, hot summer afternoon.

In 1772, Joshua Sr. (Sophia's grandfather) brought his family to live at Gnadenhutten, Ohio. Joshua Sr. died in 1775. Visitors to Gnadenhutten can see his grave marker. Photo by Jane Ann Turzillo.

Chapter 2

Family-by-family, the people of Gnadenhutten filed into the meeting house, curious to find out why the bell should summon them in the middle of the afternoon. Brother Edwards, the white mission leader, was the first to arrive because he lived in the cabin next to the church. When he saw Sophia and Thomas ringing the bell, he scolded them.

"Thomas! Sophia! It is hours yet till the evening service. You must not ring the church bell except to call the Brethren to worship."

Sophia explained: "Thomas and I saw Captain Pipe and his warriors at the river. They are painted for war and heading this way. Thomas and I rang the bell to warn the village."

"We have nothing to fear Sophia, Thomas. Pipe is ruthless, but he is not a fool. He has friends and relatives among us here at Gnadenhutten. Our bell should toll only for the glory of God, not for the fear of men," said Brother Edwards.

Sophia was ashamed. It had been, after all, her idea to ring the bell as a warning. Beside her, Thomas spoke: "Brother Edwards, our people are in danger from Pipe and his men. Twice in the past week, Pipe's warriors have shot at Brother Heckewelder as he traveled between Gnadenhutten and New Schoenbrunn. The braves say they mistook him for game, but no one believes that. Pipe and his warriors want to kill us so that we will be out of their way as they help the Red Coat British fight the Long Knives Americans."

"Thomas, hold your tongue. God is watching over us. We are safe. Now take your seats, Thomas, Sophia, and be quiet now. I will address the congregation."

"God helps he who helps himself," Thomas muttered angrily, as he sat down on the bench beside Sophia.

The church was filled now. The villagers buzzed with anxiety as they waited for the news. Brother Edwards held up his hands for silence and asked the people to be seated on the benches that were lined up before the altar. Then he spoke:

"Brethren of Gnadenhutten! The peace of God be with you. Sophia and Thomas have seen Captain Pipe and his warriors, painted for war, and heading for Gnadenhutten.

"Captain Pipe is no friend to us, as you all know, but he would not harm us. God is watching over us, we have nothing to fear. We will welcome Captain Pipe to Gnadenhutten on this day, as we welcome all travelers who pass through our town.

"I ask you, Brethren, to remember our laws. Give Chief Captain Pipe and his followers shelter for the night if they wish it. Prepare food if they are hungry, for we turn no one away who is in need.

"Now let us pray and ask for God's help."

Sophia bowed her head and shut her eyes but she couldn't concentrate on Brother Edwards' prayer. She sat on the hard bench beside her friend Thomas, head bowed, but she only pretended to pray. Outside she heard the sound of the warriors' horses as they thundered into the main street of Gnadenhutten. A sense of foreboding so strong gripped her that she swayed on her seat. Something very bad was about to happen, she sensed it, and she had the urge to run from the church, run from the village, run deep into the cool, green forest for safety. But she knew she could not, must not, for here in Gnadenhutten were her family and her friends, and whatever became of them would become of her too.

Sophia opened her eyes as the prayer ended. In the open doorway stood Captain Pipe, the dreaded leader of the Delaware braves she had seen at the river. Pipe's head was shaved, except for a single lock of black hair which hung down his back. He was wearing only a loincloth and moccasins, and his muscled body was painted with red and black slashes. In his hand he carried a tomahawk from which dangled two blond scalps.

"Edwards!" shouted Pipe. "I have returned. Many warriors follow. We are here to remove the Christian Indians from this valley. You sit in the path of the war between our enemy the Long Knives and our friend the Red Coats. Pack your belongings and leave this place!"

Brother Edwards replied, "Captain Pipe, we welcome you to Gnadenhutten. Please come inside with your helpers, so that we can all hear your words."

Pipe and two of his braves stepped inside. Through the open window, Sophia could see many warriors, many more than she and Thomas had seen at the river. They had probably been camped in the woods, awaiting Pipe's orders. How many more were waiting there still, Sophia wondered.

"Friends! Relatives!" Pipe said to the congregation, shaking his tomahawk to emphasize his words. "You say you wish to live in peace and worship what is good. Here, you cannot do this! Your lives are in danger here from the guns of the Long Knives. You must pack your belongings and follow us to a place of safety," declared Pipe.

"Captain Pipe, I have met with Brother Zeisberger at New Schoenbrunn and Brother Heckewelder at Salem. We have talked about your wish for the Brethren to leave this Muskingum Valley. All together we have almost 400 souls in the three mission towns on the Muskingum. We are not prepared to desert our towns, for it is only August and not yet time for our harvest. We cannot leave this valley before the harvest or we will starve during the winter," said Brother Edwards.

"You are all fools, Edwards," spat out Pipe. "Go now, or you will not live long enough to need the corn you wait to harvest. If you stay, the Long Knives will cut you down and blood will flow in the Muskingum. Edwards, you will come with us now to speak with Chief Pomoacan who councils with the other men who wear the black robes." Suddenly, Pipe threw his tomahawk at Brother Edwards. The tomahawk landed in the plank at Brother Edwards' feet, the two scalps swaying from its carved handle. Then two of Pipe's braves seized Brother Edwards and led him out of the meeting house. Stunned, the Brethren filed out into the blazing August sunshine after their leader.

From the congregation, Sophia's father, Josua, stepped forward to speak to Brother Edwards. Josua was Brother Edwards' Native Helper, and an important leader among the Brethren in Gnadenhutten. Sophia was proud that her father was one of the wise ones that the others looked up to.

Josua and Brother Edwards spoke briefly, and then Josua raised his hand for silence. He said to them, "Do nothing, Brethren. Go back to your homes. Brother Edwards will council with the Chiefs and the other missionary leaders, and he will be back to lead the evening worship."

The Braves lifted Brother Edwards onto a horse and Captain Pipe led the party out of the town in a whirlwind of dust. In the distance, Sophia heard the low roll of thunder.

Chapter 3

The air was full of the droning of insects. The stench of rotting flesh was overpowering. Sophia brushed off a fly that had landed on her arm, and suppressed the urge to gag. She knew that the fly had recently fed off the putrid, decaying flesh of the Gnadenhutten livestock that lay rotting in the streets.

It had been a week since Pipe had taken Brother Edwards to council. The missionaries from the neighboring villages of New Schoenbrunn and Salem had also been taken to council. The negotiations were held at the camp of the Wyandot Chief, Pomoacan. At the urging of the British, Chiefs Pipe and Pomoacan and their followers tried to convince the missionaries to take their converts and abandon the villages "for their own safety." But the missionaries resisted. It was now September 8, still too early to harvest their food supply for the winter. They could not, would not, abandon their villages.

In the last week, the warriors of Pipe and Pomoacan had harassed the converts and plundered the village of Gnadenhutten, hoping to wear down the villagers' resistance while their missionary leaders were away. The warriors had killed most of the livestock, including the chickens, cattle and pigs, leaving their carcasses to rot in streets. The citizens of Gnadenhutten were forbidden to remove the stinking mess.

The warrior Indians ransacked most of the mission homes, taking what they wanted of the clothing, blankets and household utensils. They had slit open mattresses looking for hidden items and worst of all, they had ruined much of the cornfields, and corn was the most important food at Gnadenhutten. At Gnadenhutten, the Brethren ate fresh corn fried and roasted. The surplus crop was dried and then ground for making mush, bread and pancakes. But now, the corn crop that would have fed them for the coming winter had been trampled down by the warriors' horses.

Sophia sat in her family's wood cabin with her mother and her two older sisters, Anna and Bathsheba. Her father and some of the other Native Helpers of the missionaries had been summoned to Pipe's camp outside of Gnadenhutten for the negotiations.

Fifteen-year-old Bathsheba was complaining, as usual. "The smell is making me sick, Mother. And it's stifling hot in here. Can't we go down to the river for some air? I don't think I can stand it in here another moment," said Bathsheba.

Her mother was grinding corn for the evening meal. Beside her on the work table was a cabbage Sophia had harvested from the family garden. The cabbage was all that was left of the vegetables that she and her sisters had so carefully planted and tended through the summer. In another month, the pumpkins, turnips, beans, squash and cabbages would have been ripe and ready for winter storage. In the past week, Pipe's men had stripped the crops from most of the gardens in Gnadenhutten. Sophia felt lucky to have found the one small, hard cabbage that was left in her family's garden.

"It is not safe for you to go outside while Pipe's men are camped by the river," said her Mother to Bathsheba. "We will bide our time inside until night falls. Then you and your sisters may go together to the river for water.

Surely Brother Edwards and your father will return to us soon, and this will all end."

Bathsheba heaved a sigh and threw herself down on the rough wooden bench beside Sophia and seventeen-year-old Anna. The two girls were rubbing bear fat into sheets of paper. When the paper absorbed enough of the grease, it became nearly transparent. Later, the girls would tack the paper over the window openings to replace the glass panes shattered by Pipe's warriors. The paper would block the evening breezes that were so welcome at the end of a hot day, but it would also keep out the awful smell of the rotting animals.

"You can help us with this, Bathsheba," said Sophia to her sister. "We have lots of paper."

"Whew!" said Bathsheba, wrinkling her nose in disgust. "I don't want to make windows in this heat. Besides, it hurts my arm, rubbing all that stinky fat. You and Anna do it--it was your idea."

Sophia and Anna exchanged a look. Anna smiled at Sophia and put a finger to her lips, warning her youngest sister to say nothing. When Bathsheba was in one of her moods, the slightest provocation could set off a tantrum. Bad enough to endure the heat and stink of the cabin, let alone one of Bathsheba's temper fits.

Anna tried to change the subject. "Isaac says that the British think we mission Indians are helping the Americans. That is why Captain Pipe and his British friends want us to leave Gnadenhutten. They want us out of the area," said Anna. Anna and Isaac would soon be married and living in the new cabin Isaac had been working on all summer. In Gnadenhutten, each family built and owned his own home and fenced and planted his own vegetable garden. Tending the orchards outside the town was a community project though, and the harvest was divided and shared equally among the villagers. Some was sold to their neighbors for cash or trade. At Gnadenhutten, everyone--men, women, and children, white missionaries and mission Indians--worked side-by-side in the gardens and fields, for Brother Edwards told them that all people are equal in God's eyes, and all must share the tasks of living.

This summer, Anna and Isaac had received permission to marry, and as soon as their cabin was finished, there would be a wedding ceremony and a Love Feast. At Gnadenhutten and the other mission towns of Salem and New Schoenbrunn, young people must have permission from their parents and their minister in order to marry. This law was one of the nineteen statutes agreed upon by all of the citizens of the mission towns. Sophia and her family were looking forward to the wedding celebration to come.

"Isaac says Pipe is trying to save our lives by making us move. Otherwise, the warring soldiers will kill us all," Anna said.

"When the Long Knives Americans came to our town, we gave them food and shelter. When the British came, we gave them food and shelter as well. Our law states that whenever corn is needed to entertain any stranger to our town, we will provide it. Surely Pipe knows that," said her mother.

"And look at all the good our law did for us. Now all of our livestock is gone. Our corn and vegetables are not harvested. And what food we might have stored for winter is now in the bellies of Pipe and his men," said Bathsheba.

Anna put a hand on Bathsheba's arm, "Take heart sister, all is not gone. We have some food stored. Much of our corn has already been taken in. And the fall hunt this year will provide meat for winter. God has always looked over us at Gnadenhutten, and He will provide for us this winter."

Bathsheba snatched away her arm from Anna's touch and glared at her older sister, embarrassed. Sophia giggled, glad that Anna had taken Bathsheba down a peg, but Sophia's giggle rankled Bathsheba into renewed anger. Before Bathsheba could retort, the cabin door burst open and their father, Josua, and Isaac stepped inside. The looks on their faces chilled Sophia, even though the air inside the cabin was stifling. Anna stood and went to Isaac. Sophia's father spoke:

"Pack our belongings. Brother Edwards and the other missionaries have been taken captive. The Helpers have been sent to all three mission towns to spread the news. We must abandon Gnadenhutten, Salem and Schoenbrunn at dawn tomorrow. Captain Pipe says he will lead us to a safe village to the northwest, on the Sandusky River. Our missionary leaders will travel with us. Brother Edwards says we must take what we can carry, for we may not be able to return to Gnadenhutten for a very long time."

The Cooper's House, reconstructed at Gnadenhutten. This building marks the site where Sophia lived with her family before they were taken to Captives Town. Photo by Jane Ann Turzillo.

Chapter 4

I won't carry your dumb bonnet, Sheba. There isn't a bit more room in this pack," said Sophia to her sister. Bathsheba was being difficult--again.

"You have to make room, Sophia. Look, there's plenty of space. You just haven't packed these dresses properly. Please try, Sophie. For me?" said Bathsheba in the sweet voice she only used when she was trying to get her way. "You know what awful earaches I get if I don't wear a bonnet, and this one matches my calico dress perfectly."

They were leaving Gnadenhutten. Brother Edwards and the Helpers had instructed all the householders to pack up their food and belongings. Captain Pipe and Pomoacan and their warriors were to escort them to a new settlement on the Sandusky River. The journey would take about three weeks.

"I believe the arrangement to be only temporary," said Brother Edwards at the morning worship. "Captain Pipe will escort us to our new town so that we will be out of harm's way. When the danger has passed, we will return to Gnadenhutten."

Now Sophia and Bathsheba were helping their mother pack the family belongings. Anna had gone to help Isaac pack his things as soon as worship was over. Josua was working in the orchards, gathering apples and peaches, although it would be days before the fruit was fully ripe. The clothing was tightly rolled into blanket packs, light enough to carry. Other items, such as tools and some of the food, was already packed into wooden barrels made by her father, Josua. Like his father before him, Josua was a cooper by trade, and spent much of his day making wooden barrels and containers for all who needed such items in Gnadenhutten and the other mission towns in the valley.

Sophia looked around the half-empty cabin dismayed. "Mother, we've packed all that we can carry, all that we will need for the journey and for a short stay. But look at all that we must leave behind!" said Sophia.

Most of the cooking implements had been packed, but one iron skillet still hung over the big stone fireplace. Above, on the mantle, were two pewter cups and a container of salt. Most of their clothing would be left behind in the wood chest, under the bed in which Sophia's parents slept. Some of her father's tools were stacked in the corner still waiting to be packed--most would be stored in the cellar hole beneath the cabin.

"Why, there's no room left and we've not packed father's cooper's mallet," said Sophia. The heavy wooden tool that Josua used to bend the metal barrel rings stood in the corner, next to the hearth. Josua was a skilled cooper. Nearly every family in the mission towns of Gnadenhutten and nearby Salem and New Schoenbrunn had a bucket or barrel made by Josua. Surely, they must take the mallet with them to the new village, no matter how heavy or awkward the thing was to pack.

"Daughter, we must first make sure that we have enough food and blankets and clothing for the journey. Of course, we must carry some tools to help us build what we need once we arrive at our new home. With the tools we have already packed, your father can make another mallet. The rest of our things, we will store in the cellar hole or wrap in a blanket and bury in the woods. When we return to Gnadenhutten, we will dig up our belongings," explained Sophia's mother. "Sophie, you may take the mallet to the cellar now. It should be safe there, for who else but a cooper would have use of such a tool," she added.

"Well, I still think we should take more blankets, Mother. It's bad enough that we have to travel at all, but we'll be sleeping on the hard ground until we reach the Sandusky village. It is September, and you know how cold it can get in the middle of the night," whined Bathsheba.

"You can take another blanket then, Sheba," said her mother. "If you want to carry it yourself."

That night, Sophia lay without blankets on top of her bed inside the sweltering cabin. Beside her, Anna and Bathsheba slept deeply, tired from the hard work of sorting and packing. The girls had removed the greased paper that covered the windows during the day, and every so often a breeze swept the room in which she slept--and with it the unwelcome smell of the rotting cattle which still hadn't been removed from the street.

Sophia already missed the peaceful and well-ordered life her family had known in Gnadenhutten. She loved her home of course, the sturdy cabin in which she had been born and lived all her life. She would miss going to school, too. The missionaries placed great emphasis on education, and every boy and girl in the village learned how to read at a very early age. Brother Zeisberger had carefully compiled a spelling book for the use of all the school children in the missionary villages on the Muskingum. The book contained words in both the English and the Delaware Indian language, and most of the children, including Sophia and Thomas, spoke the two languages fluently.

Sophia wondered if they would be able to continue their hymn singing when they reached their new town, for music was a very important part of worship for the Moravian Brethren. Each person in the congregation belonged to a choir grouped according to age, sex and marital status. The choir was such an important social unit to the Brethren that when a person died, he or she was buried, feet pointing East, in the choir plot, rather than a family plot of the nearby cemetery.

And what would happen to the village itself, wondered Sophia. Gnadenhutten, which meant "Tents of Grace," had stood as a civilized town in the middle of the wilderness, with comfortable cabins, tilled fields, and domesticated animals fenced in for security and protection. Now their fields were ruined, their animals slaughtered, their homes ransacked. And all because the town lay in the path of the warring British and Americans.

As she drifted into sleep, Sophia willed herself to count her blessings. Her family was safe here in the cabin with her, and she could hear the rhythmic breathing of Bathsheba sleeping soundly beside her. Their possessions, those not stolen by Pipe's warriors, were all packed for the journey they would begin together tomorrow. Other things were stored safely, awaiting their return to their beloved Gnadenhutten whenever the fighting should end. Everything was taken care of as it should be, thought Sophia, except for one thing. And that thought sent her creeping from the bed out into the night.

"Psst, Thomas. Are you awake?" Sophia whispered underneath the open window of the cabin in which Thomas lived with his parents. She heard someone move inside the cabin. Sophia stood up and peeked over the window still, and she saw Thomas rise from the platform on which he slept. Thomas' parents still slept soundly on platforms at the opposite end of the one-room cabin. Thomas crept quietly to the window, where Sophia stood."

"Sophie, you should be sleeping. We leave at dawn," he hissed, squinting at her. She sure was glad to see him.

"I need your help, Thomas. We have to save the meeting house bell. If we leave it here, the soldiers will take it. Come out and help me get up on the meeting house roof. We'll take the bell on the journey with us and give it to Brother Edwards when we reach the Sandusky village," whispered Sophia.

Thomas was fully awake now. "What about Pipe and his warriors? They'll kill us if they see," said Thomas. But he was already climbing over the window sill to join his friend.

"Sh. Just be quiet. Captain Pipe doesn't enjoy the smell of rotten meat any more than we do. He and his warriors are camped in the woods," said Sophia. The two children hurried toward the meeting house, careful to stay in the shadow line of the woven wood fences that bounded the town. Once, a dog barked at them, thinking that they were deer or raccoon, come to raid what was left of the gardens. But when the dog recognized them, she wagged her tail and went away.

When they reached the meeting house, the moon was high enough to light the cupola that sheltered the bell. "I'll go up. I'm smaller and quicker," said Sophia.

Thomas boosted Sophia up to the window sill, and handed her his knife. Quickly and quietly, she scaled the outside wall of the meeting house, until she was on the roof. In the distance she could see the smoke from the warriors' campfire, and beyond, she could see the waters of the Muskingum sparkling in the moonlight. She cut the rope that secured the bell, and lowered it down to Thomas.

Coming down from the roof was more difficult, and Sophia jumped as soon as her feet reached the level of Thomas' head. Thomas caught her around the waist as her feet touched the ground. "I'll pack the bell in the barrel with the corn we're taking on the journey," said Sophia. "I'll bury it deep in the barrel, with the corn all around it. No one will know. Then we'll surprise everyone when we reach the new village."

Thomas agreed, "It's a good plan. Brother Edwards will be pleased." Then he took off his shirt and wrapped it around the clapper to keep the bell from ringing as they crept back through the shadows to Sophia's cabin.

ESSAY

OF A

Delaware-Indian and *Engliſh*

SPELLING-BOOK,

FOR THE

USE OF THE SCHOOLS

OF THE

CHRISTIAN INDIANS
on *Muſkingum River.*

By DAVID ZEISBERGER,
MISSIONARY among the *Weſtern Indians.*

❦

PHILADELPHIA,

Printed by HENRY MILLER. 1776.

As a Moravian Indian child, Sophia was probably better educated than many of the white colonials of her time. The missionary David Zeisberger compiled a spelling book that contained both English and Delaware translations of words, prayers and other teachings. This is the cover of the speller Sophia used as a student. Courtesy of Arthur W. McGraw.

KI Wetochemelenk, talli epian Awossagame. Mawchelendasutsch Ktellewunsowoagan. Ksakimawoagan pejewigetsch. Ktelitebewoagan legetsch talli Achquidhackamike, elgiqui leek talli Awossagame. Milineen eligischbquik gunigischbuk Achpoan. Woak miwelendammauwineen 'n Tschannauchsowoagannena, elgiqui niluna miwelendammauwwenk nik Tschetschanilawequengik. Woak katschi 'npawuneen li Achquetschiechtowoaganüng, tschukund ktennineen untschi Medhicküng. Alod knihillatamen Ksakimawoagan, woak Ktallewussowoagan, woak Ktallowilissowoagan ne wuntschi hallemiwi li hallamagamik. Amen.

Metellen endcheleneyachgat Wtachpawewoagannall.

Netamicchen Wtachpawewoagan.

KATSCHI a pili Gopatamawossemiwon ni elinquechinak.

Nischbeleneyachgiechbüng Wtachpawewoagan.

Katschi a gemannibawon temiki M'sink woak temiki köcu elinaquo, nen wbockung Awossagame, tschita backing Achquidhackamike, tschita ne 'mbink equiwi backing eteek.

Mattatsch kpatamottamowunall, woaktschatta gemikindamowunall; 'ntitechquo ni Nibilalan Kpatamauwos 'nkinsi ni Getanettowit, nan netonamauwat Amemensall Ochwall Pallawewoaganall Sbacki nacha woak newo anhocqui gischgit nik Schingalitschik;

The LORD's Prayer.

OUR Father which art in Heaven. Hallowed be thy Name. Thy Kingdom come. Thy Will be done in Earth as it is in Heaven. Give us this Day our daily Bread. And forgive us our Trespasses, as we forgive them that trespass against us. And lead us not into Temptation, but deliver us from Evil. For thine is the Kingdom, and the Power, and the Glory, for ever and ever. Amen.

The Ten COMMANDMENTS.

The First Commandment.

THOU shalt have no other Gods before me.

The Second Commandment.

Thou shalt not make unto thee any graven Image, or any Likeness of any Thing, that is in Heaven above, or that is in the Earth beneath, or that is in the Water under the Earth.

Thou shalt not bow down thyself to them, nor serve them; for I the Lord thy God am a jealous God, visiting the Iniquity of the Fathers upon the Children unto the third and fourth Generation of them that hate me; and shewing Mercy unto

Facing pages from the Delaware and English speller, compiled by Zeisberger, printed in 1776. Courtesy of Arthur W. McGraw.

Chapter 5

A t dawn, September 11, 1781, the people of Gnadenhutten went to the meeting house to pray for God's guidance on their journey. For the first time in nine years, the bell did not call the worshipers to prayers. Most of the people thought that the warriors had stolen the bell. Only Sophia and Thomas knew that it was safe, packed inside one of the food barrels that would travel by canoe to its destination.

They were led on their journey by Chief Pomoacan and his Wyandot warriors--first the Salem congregation, then the Gnadenhutten congregation, then the New Schoenbrunn congregation. The three beautiful little towns on the Muskingum were abandoned. Some traveled by canoe with the supplies, but most would make the long journey on foot, taking with them what livestock the hostile Indians had not killed.

In all, about 400 Moravian Indians made the journey, along with their beloved white missionary leaders and their families. Only their captors rode horses, many of the animals stolen from the Moravians. The Delaware Indian Chief, Captain Pipe, and his men rode along behind to make sure none of the refugees escaped along the journey. But some found the journey too hard, and after saying good-bye to their missionary leaders, they slipped off into the forest under cover of the night. These people would join friends or relatives living in Indian villages.

From Gnadenhutten, the refugees followed a land trail south along the Muskingum River (Tuscarawas) to the town of Goschachgunk (Coshocton); then the trail followed the Walhonding River northwest. Those who had canoes went by water following the land trails, carrying much of the food and supplies carefully packed in the watertight barrels made by Josua. At night, the water travelers pulled their canoes ashore and made camp, waiting for the others who walked.

Sophia and her family made the journey by foot. Though the September days were warm and bright, the nights were cold and frosty and the refugees were too tired at the end of the day's walk to build even a rough lean-to. Usually, they slept on the hard ground, sharing what blankets they had brought with them. They foraged and hunted for food along the way, and shared equally the food they had brought with them from the towns. During the day, they ate pemmican, a mixture of cornmeal and water. It was tasteless, but very filling, and they thanked God for providing them.

During the second week of the journey, it began to rain. It rained steadily day and night. The refugees tried to dry out their clothing each night before the campfire, but it was soaked again in the morning, usually before they had even walked a mile. Some of the children began to cough and sniffle.

Sophia forgot about the bell. All of her time and thoughts were concentrated on keeping warm and dry. And then one night disaster struck. The captives had traveled through a steady downpour most of that day, hoping to reach the headwaters of the Kokosing before dusk. That night, Sophia helped her father pull the canoe loaded with supplies up onto the bank of the Walhonding. She and Josua unloaded the heavy barrels from the canoe, lining them up well above the shoreline so they wouldn't get wet. Then they overturned the canoe, propping it on some branches at each end. After they ate their pemmican, flavored with nuts that Anna had found along the trail, the little family crawled under the overturned canoe, which kept off the worst of the rain.

It had been raining for five days without a letup. Surely, it would stop soon, Sophia thought as she lay under the canoe, wrapped in a damp blanket. As he did every night since leaving Gnadenhutten, Josua led the evening hymn. His clear tenor rose above the rhythmic drumming of the rain on the canoe as he sang, and before he had finished one verse, others nearby joined in the singing:

> *Now thank we all our God*
> *With heart and hands and voices*
> *Who wondrous things hath done*
> *In whom His world rejoices*
> *Who from our mother's arms*
> *Hath blest us on our way*
> *With countless gifts of love*
> *And still is ours today*

Sophia's mind spiraled up, up toward consciousness, and she became aware of the water soaking her blanket. The rain was falling in a stream from the overturned canoe, wetting her feet. She opened her eyes. Beside her, Bathsheba still slept, and even though it was dark, she could make out the forms of Anna and her parents, also still asleep. What had awakened her?

She turned her head to get her bearings in the dark, wet night. The fire had burned out, and not even a coal glowed in the darkness. In the distance, she could hear the sound of the rushing Walhonding River, swollen from the rain. The river sounded closer than she remembered. And she heard something else, a hollow "thunking" sound, and voices, lots of them, shouting in alarm. The barrels! The barrels are being washed away!

Sophia roused her family, and they rushed through the downpour to the river. While they slept, the Walhonding had overflowed its banks, reaching the food and supplies that had been taken out of the canoes that afternoon. Along the river bank now, some were holding torches, and Sophia saw people in the river, struggling to retrieve the boxes and barrels that the flood had claimed. Sophia looked for the barrels she and her father had unloaded. There had been five of them--loaded with tools, food, clothing and utensils the family would need once they were settled--and of course, the bell. In the flickering torch light, Sophia saw all five, half submerged in the turbulent water, but still there.

"Get torches!" Josua said to his wife and Anna. "Sophia, Sheba! Come help me move the barrels to higher ground."

The water roared. Josua waded into the swirling water and debris so that he could get underneath the barrels and lift them out of the water. He turned one barrel onto its side, but the turbulent water spun it out of his hands and it quickly floated away in the current.

"Our clothes! And our blankets!" cried Bathsheba. Josua wasted no time watching the lost barrel float away. He turned to the next one. "We must save our food and our tools, daughters. Quickly! Help me with the others." Anna and her mother had returned with the torches. Sophia and Bathsheba went into the water and gripped the top of the second barrel. This was the barrel filled with corn. In this barrel, Sophia had hidden the Gnadenhutten bell. It was heavy and rough in her cold, wet hands, and it hurt to lift it.

Beside Sophia, her sister gasped, "I can't get a grip, it's too heavy. Let it go father, and let's get the others."

"No, we have to save this barrel," shouted Sophia, and she waded into the river up to her waist. The water quickly soaked through her long skirts, weighing her down. Sophia held on to the top of the barrel for dear life. Something heavy hit the backs of her knees, and Sophia lost control of her legs. She held on to the top of the barrel as the angry current twisted her body, but she kept her grip.

Josua saw what was happening, and shouted to his youngest child, "Don't let go." Josua and Bathsheba were both waist deep in the water now, trying to get a grip on Sophia. Josua ducked under the surface in order to get a better grasp of the bottom of the barrel, and Bathsheba pushed the barrel towards the shore at the same time. Sophia felt the barrel topple, and suddenly her face, her whole body was under the water. And then just as suddenly, her father had her by the waist and out of the water. She opened her eyes and saw her mother and Anna helping Bathsheba roll the barrel out of the water to safety.

The next day, they took stock of their belongings. Sophia and her family had saved three of their five supply barrels. They had their tools and most of their kitchen pots and utensils. They had saved their corn, and of course, the bell. They had lost most of their bedding and clothing and some of the tools they would need to build and to plant seeds in the spring. Other families lost far more. When they got to the village on the Sandusky, they would divide all that was left, equally among them.

Finally they reached the headwaters of the Kokosing, where they pulled the canoes out of the water and carried everything overland until they reached the Sandusky River. The trip took 20 days and 20 nights of unspeakable hardship for both young and old. On October first, they arrived at Old Sandusky Town, an abandoned Wyandot village. At once, the people of Gnadenhutten, Salem and New Schoenbrunn together began to build a meeting house and enough smaller houses to shelter them for the coming winter.

The mission house reconstructed at Gnadenhutten. On this site the Moravian congregation met twice a day for both religious and social events. Photo by Jane Ann Turzillo.

Map design by Karen Andrews, Kent State University.

Chapter 6

The refugees hoped that once they reached a permanent settlement, their captors would leave them in peace. But that was not the case. Pipe, Pomoacan and the warrior Indians continued to oversee their activities, keeping an especially close eye on the white missionaries, Brothers Edwards, Zeisberger and Heckewelder.

In spite of the harassment of their captors, they began to build quickly. Their new town was a disappointment. Only a few ramshackle huts remained of the old Wyandot village. Even with repairs, these structures could house only a few families. New homes must be built to shelter the rest of the families before the snows came. These homes were made of saplings bent in an upside down U, with the ends buried in the ground. More saplings were woven horizontally between the uprights, and the whole structure was covered with bark. In Gnadenhutten, Salem and New Schoenbrunn, the Moravian Brethren Indians had lived in tightly constructed log homes with shingled roofs and large fireplaces. But since their new village was to be only temporary, they would not construct log homes here.

Construction began immediately on the meeting house, which would house the missionaries and their families. From the meeting house, the missionaries would preach their sermons twice a day. This structure would also serve as a school, for all the children at Gnadenhutten had attended school during the winter months, learning to read and write and count. They refused to name their town, calling the place Captives Town.

They had been at Captives Town for nearly a week before Sophia spoke again with Thomas. Now she hurried to catch up with him as he walked to the meeting house.

"Thomas, I've missed you," she said to her friend, her breath steaming from her lips in the cold October air. "We have something important to talk about."

"Sophia! How good to see you. Your parents are well? And your sisters?" asked Thomas.

"Well enough," she answered. "Mother has a cold, and father is fine. Since the Red Coat soldiers arrived, Father spends all of his time with Brother Edwards and the other Helpers. They have much to talk about, he says. Anna is happy--she has her Isaac. And Bathsheba--well, you know Sheba. She has much to complain about these days," said Sophia.

Thomas gave her a sideways look that told her he knew what she meant.

"Thomas, the meeting house is finished. And most of the houses are done now, too. Each day, when I take our supper corn from the barrel, I get closer to uncovering the bell. The corn barrel is almost empty. Do you think now is the time to give the bell to brother Edwards?"

They reached the meeting house. From where they stood, they could see Captain Pipe and a few of his braves talking to two men in bright red uniforms, two of the recently arrived British Red Coat soldiers. Long, shiny sabers hung from their belts, and they all carried rifles slung across their backs. More Red Coats waited in the large boat anchored near the village. Josua told her that the boat had crossed the big Lake Erie to the mouth of the Sandusky.

The children watched Pipe and the British soldiers as they laughed and talked. Then one of the soldiers took a flask from inside his jacket and offered it to Captain Pipe, who drank from it and wiped his mouth with the back of his hand.

"The British bring rum--and more trouble I'm afraid. I am worried, Sophia," said Thomas. Then he turned to her, took her hand and said, "Keep the bell hidden, Sophie. If we hang the bell in the meeting house now, Pipe or the Red Coats might steal it and melt it down for bullets." Sophia agreed. That night, Thomas and Sophia took the bell out of the corn barrel. Carefully, they coated the bell with bear grease, and then they buried it in the woods for safekeeping.

Each morning, Sophia helped her mother prepare the family's main meal of the day. They cooked outside over an open cook fire, but they ate their meals inside their bark hut, where it was warmer. Now, Sophia stirred the fragrant concoction that simmered in the iron cooking pot suspended over the fire. Today they would eat stew. Yesterday, Josua had traded some of their corn for a bit of meat, the first flesh they had eaten since they left Gnadenhutten. Sophia's stomach grumbled in hungry anticipation. Soon it would be the hunting season, and there would be plenty of meat for everyone in Captives Town--that is, if Pipe and the British let them go on a hunt. There certainly wasn't enough corn and vegetables to feed all of them during the coming winter. Surely Pipe wouldn't let his own kin starve, thought Sophia. Pipe was a Delaware, just like most of the Indians living here in Captives Town.

Inside the hut, her mother coughed. Later, Sophia would brew her a soothing tea from the roots she had gathered this morning. She thought about it as she stirred the stew. Sophia wished her father would hurry home so the family could eat. As a Helper, Josua's opinion was much valued by the community, especially the missionaries, and Josua was in conference with them now as he had been for most of the week.

It was well after noon before Josua returned to his family, and he brought news that spoiled Sophia's appetite for the fragrant stew she had tended all morning. Josua entered the low door of the bark hut and sat down beside his wife and daughters. "The British have taken our missionaries to the big boat, and they are being held captive. Brother Edwards, Brother Zeisberger and Brother Heckewelder are accused of helping the Long Knives in the war with the Red Coats. Our missionaries deny these charges, of course.

"Moravian Christians take no sides in war, we work only for peace. But the Red Coats and Captain Pipe have orders to escort our missionaries and their Helpers to Detroit for a trial. The charge is treason. The Helpers are to join the missionaries on the boat at once. I've come to say good-bye," said Josua.

Chapter 7

Sophia and Bathsheba sat huddled together for warmth, waiting for Anna and their mother to return from the storehouse where the community's food was kept. The dwindling food supply was carefully rationed at Captives Town. Once a day, someone from each family was sent to receive the day's meal.

Sophia heard her mother coughing outside the hut, a violent rasping cough that worried her. Anna and Mother entered, quick to fasten down the blanket that served for a door to the bark hut in which they had now lived for six months. A few snowflakes floated in with them, and spiraled with the air current before they melted.

"Another squall approaches," said Sophia's mother, hoarsely. Sophia's heart sank. Winter at Captives Town was much different than winter in the towns on the Muskingum Valley where the snow came quietly, covering the earth in a deep blanket of white. Here, the snow came with wind, whipping and blowing down from the big Lake Erie. Sometimes in a squall, you couldn't see your own hand held right in front of your face. At least the squalls were short-lived.

"What did you get for our meal, mother," asked Bathsheba, who was sitting on the floor, wrapped in a blanket. The hut offered protection from the wind, if not from the bitter cold.

"A bit of corn meal and some potatoes," said her mother, as she took the packet of food out from under her wrappings. Sophia saw that there was barely enough food to feed one person, let alone four hungry people who hadn't eaten anything since the day before. Bathsheba stood and took the food from her mother.

"These potatoes are moldy, Mother. They will make us sick. What else did you bring? Surely you have more food?" whined Bathsheba.

"We'll cut off the mold, Sheba," said Anna, who took the small vegetables from her and began to prepare the meal. "We can make corn cakes and roast them with the potatoes in the campfire. Isaac says that Indians from the next village will be here to trade tomorrow. They will have food. Isaac says that we must be careful, though. We must not trade with the warrior Indians because their goods were stolen from those they killed."

"Isaac says. Isaac says. Does Isaac know everything, Anna? Can't you think for yourself?" Spat out Bathsheba at her older sister. "The fact is, we are running out of food and we have very little left to trade with. We're all going to starve here in this God forsaken place," said Bathsheba. "We'll just have to trade with anyone who has food, and never mind what Isaac says."

Mother put her hand on Bathsheba's arm, and said gently "Our laws say that we will not go to war nor will we trade with warriors. We will observe our laws here at Captives Town just as we did at Gnadenhutten. God has not forsaken us, nor this place, daughter." Her voice was weak and shaky. Sophia took off her blanket and put it on her mother's shoulders.

"I will help Anna with the meal, mother. When it is cooked, we will ask God's blessing and then we'll eat," said Sophia. Her mother smiled at her and then was seized by a terrible cough that lasted a very long, long time.

"Mother needs medicine," said Sophia to her sisters the next day. They had all been awakened in the night by their mother's frequent coughing. Now Mother lay in the hut, wrapped in a blanket, her eyes closed, her face flushed with fever.

"And we all need more food. If we don't eat more, we'll all get sick, and then who will take care of us?" asked Bathsheba, as she poked at the campfire outside the hut.

"The snow has stopped," said Anna. "I say that we must take stock of what we have left. What we don't need to stay alive, we must show to the trading Indians from the neighboring villages. We must exchange these things for food so that we can keep up our strength until our leaders return from Detroit," said Anna. Bathsheba and Sophia agreed to the plan.

That afternoon they took stock of their belongings. They had an extra cooking pot, two blankets, and a few storage barrels that had been skillfully made by Josua. They also decided to trade most of their extra clothing, though this decision did not please Bathsheba.

"We'll need our dresses to keep warm, sisters," protested Bathsheba. She was right, of course, but they needed food more than clothing now, and they might not be able to trade the other items for much of anything. Finally, Bathsheba agreed to trade one of her own dresses.

Two days later, the trading Indians came to Captives Town. It was a hard winter for everyone, not just the refugees from the Muskingum towns. Food was scarce in all the nearby villages, but Sophia and her sisters were able to trade their belongings for a few nuts, some corn and beans, and best of all, a small rabbit to stew for their dinner.

When they lived at Gnadenhutten, they had not eaten rabbit. Nor did they eat ground hogs, even though they were plentiful enough in the Muskingum Valley. Sophia once asked Thomas why he did not hunt the rabbit or the ground hog, and he had told her that those animals were the relatives of the Delaware. One did not eat one's own relatives, he had joked, when one could eat deer, bear and fish from the river. Sophia thought of his joke as she traded her best dress for the scrawny rabbit. Well, tonight she would eat rabbit, she thought, and it would taste very good, for she had not had meat for more than a week. And besides, she was not Delaware, she was Moravian.

Sophia was outside their hut later than evening, stirring the stew pot suspended over the fire, when Thomas joined her. "Thomas, you will share our meal with us tonight?" Sophia asked her friend. "We made trade today for food, and we eat yet another day."

"Ah, Sophie. Your stew smells wonderful. Yes, I'll join you and I'll sweeten the stew pot with the news I bring," said Thomas.

"Brother Edwards has returned? And my father?" asked Sophia, her heart leaping for joy.

"No, no, Sophie. Not yet. But Pomoacan has given permission for some of us to return to the Muskingum towns. We can go home! But we must return to Captives Town in a month," said Thomas. As they ate the hot, tasty stew, warmed by the blazing campfire, Thomas explained. He said that Pomoacan had given permission for 150 of the residents of Captives Town to return to their homes on the Muskingum River to gather what was left of their belongings and food supplies. Those who were young, strong and healthy should make the trip and return with supplies for those who stayed behind as hostages in Captives Town.

"I am going and so are my parents." Thomas looked at Anna. "Isaac said he will join us. Which of you will go with us?" Thomas asked Sophia and her sisters.

Sophia looked at Anna and Bathsheba, then glanced at the hut. Inside, her mother lay wrapped in blankets, weak and fevered. Mother had eaten some of the stew, and she did seem a little better for it, but she was still very sick. Mother was too weak to travel, and they could not leave her alone.

Well, I certainly want to go," said Bathsheba, "and Anna will want to go with Isaac, so you'll have to stay here, Sophia, and tend to mother. Besides, you're the youngest. It just makes sense that you should be the one to stay."

Sophia glared at Bathsheba. Sophia wanted to go too. Just think! They could go home, at least for a little while. At Gnadenhutten, Sophia could sleep in her own bed, warmed by a fire in the hearth that Josua had built. And stored in their cellar, along with Josua's cooper's tools, was food--nuts, dried fruit and strips of jerky, and pemmican--enough food to feed several families in the coming weeks. From the cellar beams hung dried medicinal herbs that could help ease her mother's cough. Sophia wanted to go to Gnadenhutten with the others and get all these things and bring them back to Captives Town.

But what about Mother? They couldn't all go and leave her here alone. One of them would have to stay behind. Why, oh why must it be me, Sophia thought desperately. Then she had an idea.

"Anna, Bathsheba, it is true that mother is not well enough to travel and one of us must stay behind. All of us are strong enough to make the trip to Gnadenhutten and back. I say we should decide by lottery who will go and who will stay," said Sophia.

Thomas laughed and clapped her on the back. "That's a wonderful idea, Sophia, and only you would have thought of it! Why not let God decide who will go and who will stay," he said, still chuckling.

The Moravian settlements often used the lottery to settle major questions that concerned the entire community. By lottery, they decided questions of elections, appointments of Helpers, and settled matters involving church policy. The method was to put three pieces of paper into a box. One piece was written "yes," on the second, "no," the third piece of paper was blank. Next, the question was asked. Then someone was appointed to draw one of the pieces of paper from the box. If the person drew the "yes," the motion was carried;' if "no," the motion was denied. If the hand drew a blank paper, the decision was postponed until a later time. Brother Edwards said that the lottery allowed God to make the decision by guiding the hand of the one who selected the piece of paper.

"But we have no paper, no box. How shall we draw lots?" asked Bathsheba. Thomas answered her, "We will draw from straw," he said and he stooped to pick up three pieces of straw from the pile used to kindle the fire and line the floor of the hut. One piece of straw, he broke into half its length.

"Each of you girls will draw a piece of straw from my hand. If you draw the short piece, you stay," said Thomas. He turned his back and arranged the straws in his hand. Then he turned around and held out the straws, first to Anna.

Anna drew the middle straw from Thomas' fist. It was long. "I go with Isaac," she said, beaming.

Then Thomas held out the remaining two straws to Sophia. Sophia held her breath as she reached out. She touched first one straw, then the other, hoping to feel some sign as to which she should draw. Finally she drew the left straw. It was short. Beside her, Bathsheba clapped her hands in joy. Bathsheba and Anna would go to Gnadenhutten. Sophia must stay in Captives Town.

Two days later, those who were to make the trip to Gnadenhutten said farewell to their friends and relatives who would remain in Captives Town. Together, they prayed for a safe journey for the travelers and for a swift return of their missionary leaders and their Helpers who were still in Detroit.

Sophia watched as her family and friends left Captives Town that day. It was a cold, crisp morning, and her breath steamed from her nostrils. She hugged herself, shivering in the early light. She had kissed both her sisters good-bye earlier, and now her eyes sought out Thomas, who was with his parents. He saw her, and ran over to where she stood.

"Keep the bell safe, Sophia," he said. "When I return we'll build a cupola for the meeting house and hang the bell. By Easter, the Gnadenhutten bell will be calling us to worship."

Sophia kissed Thomas on the cheek. "God keep you safe, Thomas. And watch over Bathsheba if you can. Anna has Isaac, but Sheba is alone," said Sophia. Thomas promised. The travelers left Captives Town on foot, taking the trail that would lead them back to their beloved home on the Muskingum. They promised to return soon--they must--for Pomoacan and his warriors held their relatives hostage in Captives Town.

That evening, after she had made her mother comfortable inside their hut, Sophia sat outside and watched the sun set. The sky was a brilliant yellow, tinged with vivid red. In the changing shapes of the clouds, Sophia watched rabbits and ground hogs frolicking across the sky, tinged golden by the rays of the setting sun, until finally they turned blood red as the sun sank below the horizon. Sophia shivered in the cold air.

Chapter 8

Sophia was hungry, but she did not cry because she knew that crying would use up what little strength she had left. Beside her, Mother coughed and coughed in spasms that shook her frail body. Sophia watched her helplessly and swallowed her tears of despair. If they were to survive, Sophia had to save her strength.

Many of the Brethren Indians in Captives Town had died over the winter--from cold and hunger and disease. Most of those who died were babies and young children. In the weeks since her sisters and the others had been gone, it had snowed continuously. The cold winds had pushed the snow drifts high against the walls of the cabins and bark huts of Captives Town, insulating the people within. But the snows had made it impossible for the Brethren to find food or wood to keep the cook fires burning. And so all were hungry. Not even the trading Indians could help them now, for all the trails were impassable.

There was no news from Detroit, where the missionaries and their Helpers, including Josua, had been taken. The British Major DePeyster thought that the Brethren had been helping the Americans in the war against the British. Sophia's mother explained that the charge was called "treason" and it was very serious indeed. If the missionaries were found guilty of the charge, they would not be able to return to their congregations. But did that mean that Sophia's father Josua would also be forbidden to return? Sophia worried that she would never see her dear father again.

All they could do is wait--wait for the missionaries and the Helpers to return from Detroit, and wait for their relatives and friends to return from Gnadenhutten. Sophia was tired of waiting. She got up and kissed her mother's damp forehead. She put her own blanket, warm from her body's heat, across her mother's shoulders. "I will go to the meeting house now, Mother; perhaps someone has shot a squirrel or a deer. If there is meat, I will bring back our share," said Sophia.

Sophia wrapped her cloak around her tightly and left the hut. She blew into her hands to warm them as she made her way the short distance to the meeting house. Others had gathered there too, and they were grouped around the embers of a dying fire smoldering in the stone hearth at one end of the building. One old woman motioned her to the fire. Sophia recognized her as Elizabeth, from New Schoenbrunn.

"Greetings, Sister Elizabeth," said Sophia. She wanted to ask immediately if there was food, but she held back for fear of being rude. After all, everyone else must be as hungry as she was.

"Dear child, join us," said Elizabeth. "You are well? And your mother?"

"Well enough, thank you. But Mother's cold worsens, and her coughing makes her too weak to sit up. I thought if there was any food for sharing today, I could make her a soothing soup," said Sophia. The others around the hearth watched her, but were silent.

"Nothing yet for food, dear girl. Maybe later. Some of our New Schoenbrunn men went hunting this morning. Come back tonight and there may be meat. I will bring you some dried mint with which to brew your mother a tea. It should help her cough," said Elizabeth. Sophia thanked her and left the meeting house. She dare not leave her mother alone for too long.

When she went back to the meeting house later, she found the building empty, the fire cold. Apparently the hunters had not been successful that day. Beside the hearth was a package wrapped in cloth, tied with a string. Sophia opened the package, and inside was the dried mint from Elizabeth. Sophia put the package inside her dress and returned to her hut.

That night, Sophia used the wooden cover of the empty corn barrel as fuel for the fire. Over the fire, she melted snow in her mother's iron kettle and when the water boiled, she added the mint leaves. Sophia and her mother asked God's blessing before their meal. Tomorrow, maybe, there would be meat.

The next morning, Sophia awoke with a start. Outside, she heard excited voices. Quickly, she sat up. Had the hunters returned with food? Or perhaps the trading Indians had arrived in Captives Town. Sophia glanced at her mother, who was still sleeping. Better let her rest, she thought. The mint tea had been soothing. Mother hadn't coughed as much during the night.

Quietly, Sophia left the hut and hurried toward the meeting house. The sun was shining, the air warm. By nightfall, most of the snow would be melted, Sophia thought. As she neared the meeting house, she could hear the excited voices inside. She stopped short. Why, she could hear laughter--a sound she had not heard for many months! Sophia started to run.

"They're back!" shouted a young boy, who hung out over the meeting house window sill. "Brother Edwards, Brother Zeisberger and Brother Heckewelder--and the Helpers, too. They are all back, and they brought supplies!" screamed the boy in his excitement. Sophia ran as fast as she could to the meeting house. The one-room building was filled with people, all shouting and laughing. More people were coming in behind Sophia and she got pushed toward the front. She stood on her tip toes and she could see the face of Brother Edwards, smiling and talking to Elizabeth. And then she spotted her father, Josua. "Father!" she shouted. "Father! Over here!" she cried, until finally Josua looked her way. And suddenly she was in the arms of her good, strong father and he held her close and whispered her name.

That night the Brethren held a Love Feast and all the people shared the food that the missionaries and their Helpers brought back from Detroit. They ate meat, vegetables, and bread made of wheat flour. After the hymn singing, they would drink coffee or hot choco-late with their sugar cake, the traditional foods of the Moravian Love Feast Celebration.

They sang hymns and thanked God that the mission-aries were acquitted of the treason charges. Josua told them that Chief Captain Pipe had spoken up for them at the trial, telling the British that the missionaries and their followers were not helping the Americans, that they were innocent of the charges. The British Colonel DePeyster believed Pipe and released the missionaries and Helpers and told them they were free to return to their people.

Sophia dreamed. She dreamed she was running, running away from something horrible that was chasing her through the dark forest. She didn't remember the forest ever being that dark. Someone was calling her name, and she turned her head, still running. Relief flooded her body! It was Bathsheba! It was her own sister chasing her through the forest. Then why was she so afraid? She stopped running and turned to greet her sister. But when the girl approached, Sophia saw that it was not Bathsheba. It was someone else wearing Bathsheba's dress, and that person had no face. The faceless figure raised a bloody tomahawk, as if to strike her. In her dream, Sophia became as small and quiet as a bird when the shadow of the hawk is on the land.

Chapter 9

Sophia walked along the path to the river. She felt lively and full of energy in the warm spring air. Mother was better now, too, thank God. The good food that the missionaries and their Helpers brought back from Detroit had been shared equally among them. Now there was enough nourishment for all until their relatives returned from Gnadenhutten.

Although her stomach was full, there was an ache in her gut that wouldn't go away. She was very worried. According to the missionary calendar, it was now March 23, 1782. More than enough time had elapsed for those who had journeyed to Gnadenhutten to have gathered their belongings and returned to Captives Town.

Sophia stooped and picked up a small stone to skip upon the river. It made her think of Thomas, and their stone skipping contests on the Muskingum. How she missed Thomas.

She tossed the stone aside and sat down on the grassy river bank. The grass smelled rich and alive. Sophia pulled off her stockings and let the sun warm her legs. She looked up at the sky and the sun made a blot on her vision when she looked away. When she closed her eyes, there was a beautiful explosion of red behind her eyelids. The day was almost perfect. Now, if only the others would come back.

Behind her, she heard a movement in the bushes that lined the path to the river. Sophia opened her eyes and turned around, hoping to see a rabbit, or maybe even a deer. Her breath caught in her throat and she stared, wondering if the sun had somehow permanently damaged her vision. There stood Thomas on the path, as if thinking about him had brought him to her. But something wasn't right. Thomas took a small step towards her and crumpled to the ground, and Sophia ran to where he lay and kneeled over his body. When she lifted his head into her lap, her hand came away sticky with blood. Horror replaced her joy at seeing her old friend. Thomas was scalped!

Brother Edwards and Josua carried Thomas back to the meeting house, where they made a bed for him in front of the hearth. Sophia's mother bathed the blood from Thomas' body and dressed him in clean clothes. Sophia helped her mother apply a soothing ointment to the raw and oozing patch of skull on the top of Thomas' head, and he fainted from the pain of it.

Now he was awake, and Sophia and her parents and Brothers Edwards and Heckewelder were anxious to hear Thomas' story. Others had come into the meeting house, and stood around the makeshift bed upon which Thomas lay. Sophia's mother held a cup of steaming herb tea to Thomas' lips. "Drink this, Thomas. It will lessen the pain," urged her mother. Thomas sipped a little of the steaming liquid.

"Thomas, tell us how this awful thing happened to you. And what of the others who went with you to Gnadenhutten?" Brother Edwards asked.

Thomas shuddered and squeezed his eyes shut, as he remembered: "When we arrived at the Muskingum, we split up into three groups. Those who had lived in Salem went there, and those who lived in New Schoenbrunn went to their homes to gather what they could. The rest of us, under the leadership of Brother Abraham, went on to Gnadenhutten. On the first day, we gathered the corn from the fields, and at night we shelled the kernels into bags so that we could carry it back to Captives Town. Some corn we buried in the woods so that we would be able to plant the fields again when we returned to Gnadenhutten. There was so much corn--much more than we expected to find.

"We also met some traveling Indians who wished to trade with us. They traded hunting rifles and clothing for our extra food, for they were very hungry and we now had plenty.

"On the second day, some of us were in the orchard, gathering what we could find there, when some Long Knives led by a Colonel Williamson surrounded us. The Long Knives led us back to town and gathered us all together. They told us to give up our knives and rifles-- that we were to go with them to Pittsburgh for our own protection. They said they would return our weapons once we reached Fort Pitt."

Thomas paused while Sophia's mother lifted a cup of hot broth to his lips. Then he continued.

"When they had all our weapons, they began to ask us questions." Thomas looked at Sophia, and reached for her hand. "Your sister, Bathsheba. They said her dress came from a white woman who was murdered by Indians the week before. They said that we must be the murderers. Bathsheba said she got the dress in a trade with the traveling Indians she had met just the day before." Though he still held her hand tightly, Thomas looked away from Sophia now, and squeezed shut his eyes. Tears fell out from under his eyelids and rolled down his cheeks, soaking the rolled up blanket on which his head was propped.

Thomas continued, but did not open his eyes. "Brother Abraham explained to the Long Knives that we came to our town only for food to take back to our starving relatives on the Sandusky.

"Colonel Williamson laughed at Brother Abraham, and he grabbed a handful of Brother Abraham's hair and pulled it out. Colonel Williamson said what a pretty head of hair he had and what a fine scalp it would be to hang from his belt." Thomas choked back his tears, and Sophia squeezed his hand tighter.

"The soldiers took all the women and children and put them in Brother Edwards' house. My mother was there. Both Anna and Bathsheba were with her. The men and boys were locked up in the meeting house, our wrists and feet bound. At dusk, those who had been working the fields at Salem were captured and imprisoned with us. They told us that in the morning we all would be killed. Only those working at New Schoenbrunn escaped the murders.

"We spent the night singing hymns and praying. Brother Abraham led us. We could hear the women singing in the next house. Sometimes, we sang together. All night, we sang and prayed, for no one could sleep. As I sang, I worked at the ropes that bound my hands and feet, and when I had freed myself I helped Jacob, who was next to me, untie his bonds. There was no more time to help any of the others. At dawn, the soldiers unlocked the doors.

"The soldiers came into the meeting house and told us to stand up and face the wall. Jacob and I were standing side-by-side next to the door, and we watched as one of the soldiers swung his weapon against the back of Brother Abraham's skull, crushing it. Then the soldier took Abraham's scalp and held it aloft as the other soldiers cheered. The same sounds were coming from the women's house.

"Jacob and I watched as the soldier killed them one by one--Tobias, Glickhikan and Israel were next. I watched them kill my own father in this way. My father's limbs were still moving when they took his scalp. Then the soldier handed his weapon to another and said to him, 'My arm hurts me now. You go on in the same way. I think I have done pretty well.' And he laughed as he walked away." Thomas was crying now, his tears soaking the pillow. Sophia took the cup of broth from her mother and held it for Thomas to drink.

"Jacob and I had tied the ropes loosely around our hands and feet to fool the soldiers. When the soldiers were watching Petrus die, we threw off the ropes and ran out through the open door. We had talked during the night about warning those still at New Schoenbrunn. Outside the cabin, were more soldiers. One of them chased us as we headed towards the woods. I got caught, but I watched Jacob run into the woods towards New Schoenbrunn. Then came pain and darkness. When I awoke, the sun was far in the western sky. I hurt all over, and blood was running in my eyes, but I kept crawling until I reached the path that leads to the woods. I could hear the soldiers laughing and joking as they set all the buildings on fire.

"I have been trying to get back here since then. I had to tell you what happened at Gnadenhutten. You had to know."

Thomas closed his eyes, his crying ceased. Sophia let go of Thomas' hand and her eyes sought her parents. They now knew the worst. Anna and Bathsheba and all the others were dead, murdered by soldiers at Gnaden-hutten. Sophia looked at her father's face, so full of sorrow, yet no tears flowed. Josua moved toward Thomas and spoke.

"Thomas, before you rest, I must ask you one more question about what happened at Gnadenhutten. By what murder weapon did our loved ones die?"

Without opening his eyes, Thomas answered, "The weapon was your own cooper's mallet, Brother Josua."

And with this knowledge came the full pain of her loss, a pain so sudden and violent that it tore the breath from Sophia's body.

Chapter 10

I t was days before those at Captives Town learned the full horror of what had happened at Gnaden-hutten on March 8, 1782. Ninety-six Moravian Indians--thirty-five men, twenty-seven women and thirty-four children had been killed and scalped by Colonel Williamson and his American soldiers. Then Williamson had ordered that the two buildings containing the bodies be burned. When they reached New Schoenbrunn, Williamson and his men found that village deserted, thanks to Jacob's warning.

In early summer, the Moravian Indians at Captives Town and their missionary leaders received an invitation from the Chippewas in Michigan to come and build a new mission north of Detroit. Colonel DePeyster offered to lend his sailing ship to transport the Moravians to the site. Sophia and her parents carefully packed their few belongings into the empty corn barrel as they prepared for the journey. At the bottom of the barrel rested the Gnadenhutten bell, recently unearthed from its hiding place in the woods.

They left Ohio country and went to Michigan. Sailing along the shores of Lake St. Clair, they entered the Huron River. From the ship, Sophia looked out over the water to take in the land that would become her new home. The land along the river was thickly overgrown with heavy timber. Hunting would be good on such land, Sophia knew. She saw a great many sugar trees and wild cherry, as well as the more common oak, poplar, walnut, hickory and ash. Although forested, the land here was very flat, not like the hilly green forests that surrounded her beloved Gnadenhutten. Sophia wondered if she would ever be able to go back to the place of her birth--and the place of the deaths of so many of her relatives and friends.

Only nineteen converts, including Sophia and her parents, sailed to Michigan with their missionary leaders. Many were too sick to travel; others, too discouraged to make a new beginning. Thomas, now fully recovered, had refused to go.

"Sophie, my friend, I will not be going with you to Michigan," he told her on the morning of our departure.

"But Thomas, surely you'll not want to stay here in Captives Town alone," she protested. "And it is not yet safe to return to our towns on the Muskingum. Where will you stay?"

"I will travel south to find my mother's people," he answered. They live in a Delaware village near Goschachgunk. I will ask them to accept me into their town," said Thomas. His eyes did not meet Sophia's, and that worried her more than Thomas' words. She took both his hands in her own.

"But Thomas, you cannot leave us. You are a Moravian," she cried, tears rolling down her cheeks.

Only then did Thomas look into her eyes. "No, Sophie. I am a Delaware." She had not seen him on the shore when the ship sailed away.

Now they had arrived at the land given to them by the Chippewas for the duration of the war between the Red Coats British and the Long Knives Americans. They chose a site on the south bank of the river on which to build their town. But first, they must plant their gardens so that there would be enough corn and vegetables to harvest in the fall. They spent four days planting turnips, lettuce, beans and other vegetables they had been given in Detroit. As they worked, they sang hymns. Twice each day according to their beliefs, they gathered for prayer and asked God's blessing on their new home. On July 27, they met to plan out their new town.

Just like their towns on the Muskingum, the new town would be laid out in a T pattern--the streets, four rods (66 feet) wide. Each family's house lot was three rods (49.5 feet) wide. They named their village New Gnadenhutten. Construction began first on the meeting house. Every man, woman and child was enlisted to help in the building.

Outside their sleeping tent, Sophia helped her father unpack his tools--the sharp saws and axes would be used to cut down the huge sassafras trees. The wood would then be cut into two-foot wide planks for the walls and floors of the buildings. Josua also had his cooper's tools for making the boxes and barrels and buckets to store their food and water. Many of the containers from Gnadenhutten had been burned for firewood during the hard winter at Captives Town--in one of the remaining corn barrels, the bell was safely stored.

"Father, will the new meeting house have a belfry?" Sophia asked Josua, as she lifted the bell from the barrel and unwrapped it. The bell gleamed in the sunshine.

Her father smiled down at her. "Sophie, your bell will toll the evening service on this very day. We will build a bell tower from which to hang it. Later, when the meeting house is finished, we can move it to the belfry," said Josua to his daughter.

Sophia embraced her father. So much had happened since the bell had last called them to worship. She had lost both her sisters, and in a way, Thomas. And she had lost all the others who would never again on this earth hear the tolling of the bell, calling them to worship.

Sophia left her father's embrace and lifted the bell. She could feel the warmth of the sun in the metal. An unaccustomed peacefulness entered her heart, a feeling that had not been there for many months. This bell was made to last, she thought. It survived, and so shall I. And one day, I will carry this bell back to Gnadenhutten where it will toll over the graves of my people who are now with Jesus.

Sophia and her father took the bell to the site of the meeting house and began to build New Gnadenhutten.

Epilogue

Rarely do we find biographical information about Indians written by their contemporaries. When we do, there is usually very little about the personal lives of the Indians, particularly the women and children. But because the Moravian missionaries kept such detailed diaries, we do have the accounts of a few individuals--among them, Sophia.

After the massacre, Sophia and her family moved seven times before they returned to the Muskingum Valley in Ohio. Sophia married James in 1797 and they had at least three children, two of whom died in infancy. Sophia died in 1801, at the age of 27, and was buried at the Goshen Mission Cemetery in Goshen Township, Tuscarawas County, Ohio. Her grave is marked with a simple stone set into the earth, hand carved with her name, Sophia Junior.

The cemetery at Goshen, Ohio, in which Sophia is buried beside her mother. The cemetery is also the final resting place of the missionary leader, David Zeisberger. Photo by Jane Ann Turzillo.

Close-up of Sophia's grave marker, inscribed Sophia Junior. Her mother's grave marker is inscribed Sophia Senior. Photo by Jane Ann Turzillo.

How Much
of This Book is True?

The massacre at Gnadenhutten and the events preceding the slaughter happened just as I have told them in this book. Those who remained at Captives Town heard about the tragedy from two boys (one of them, the Thomas of this book) who were able to escape. Zeisberger wrote: "Two well-grown boys, who saw the whole thing and escaped gave this information. One of these lay under the heaps of slain and was scalped, but finally came to himself and found the opportunity to escape... The boy who was scalped and got away, said the blood flowed in streams in the house, which was set on fire" (qtd. in Earl Olmstead's Black-coats Among the Delaware, Kent State University Press, p. 141).

The Sophia of this book was a girl of seven or eight years at the time of the Gnadenhutten massacre in the spring of 1782. From the missionary records, we know that Sophia was descended on both sides of her family from grandparents who distinguished themselves in the Indian missions of their time. Her mother's father was John Papunhank, the first Indian baptized by David Zeisberger at a mission on the Susquehanna. Sophia's father's father, Josua or Joshua Sr., a Mahican Indian, was one of the founders of the Gnadenhutten mission, and an important leader there during his lifetime. He died in 1775, and visitors can see his grave marker at Gnadenhutten today.

Anna and Bathsheba were the oldest children of Sophia Sr. and Josua Jr. They were unfortunately among those killed at Gnadenhutten in 1782. Sophia also had other brothers and sisters who are not named in this book.

Both Sophias, the girl of this story and her mother, died at Goshen, Ohio, in 1801, and are buried side-by-side, very near the grave of their beloved missionary leaders, Brothers Zeisberger and Edwards. Sophia's father died in 1806 at a mission in Indiana, where he was burned to death by the Indian, Tenskwatawa, the treacherous and disturbed brother of Tecumseh.

*Today, a plaque marks the burial spot of those massacred
at Gnadenhutten in 1782. In 1797, the missionary Heckewelder returned to the scene of the massacre, collected all
the human bones he could find, and buried them together
in this grave.* Photo by Jane Ann Turzillo.

Memorial at Gnadenhutten. Photo by Jane Ann Turzillo.

The First Laws in Ohio

L aws agreed upon by the Christian Indians of the Moravian settlements in Ohio, August 1771.

I. We will know no other God but the one only true God, who made us and all creatures, and came into this world in order to save sinners; to Him alone we will pray.

II. We will rest from work on the Lord's day, and attend public service.

III. We will honor father and mother, and when they grow old and needy we will do for them what we can.

IV. No person will get leave to dwell with us until our teachers have given their consent, and the helpers (native assistants) have examined him.

V. We will have nothing to do with thieves, murderers, whoremongers, adulterers, or drunkards.

VI. We will not take part in dances, sacrifices, heathenish festivals, or games.

VII. We will use no tshapiet, or witchcraft, when hunting.

VIII. We renounce and abhor all tricks, lies, and deceits of Satan.

IX. We will be obedient to our teachers and to the helpers who are appointed to preserve order in our meetings in the towns and fields.

X. We will not be idle, nor scold, nor beat one another, nor tell lies.

XI. Whoever injures the property of his neighbor shall make restitution.

XII. A man shall have but one wife--shall love and provide for her and his children. A woman shall have but one husband, be obedient to him, care for her children, and be cleanly in all things.

XIII. We will not admit rum or any other intoxicating liquor in our town. If strangers or traders bring intoxicating liquor, the helpers shall take it from them and not restore it until the owners are ready to leave the place.

XIV. No one shall contract debts with traders, or receive goods to sell for traders, unless the helpers give their consent.

XV. Whoever goes hunting, or on a journey, shall inform the minister or stewards.

XVI. Young persons shall not marry without the consent of their parents and the minister.

XVII. Whenever the stewards or helpers appoint a time to make fences or to perform other work for the public good, we will assist and do as we are bid.

XVIII. Whenever corn is needed to entertain strangers, or sugar for love-feast, we will contribute from our stores.

XIX. We will not go to war, and will not buy anything of warriors taken in war.

OTHER BOOKS FOR YOUNG READERS:

AUTISM--From Tragedy to Triumph. Carol Johnson and Julia Crowder. The authors tell the story of a young man, from birth to college matriculation, how Julia, the mother, coped with his illness. Illustrated. 1965-0 $12.95 p.

BETTER THAN OUR BEST--*Women of Valor in American History*. Ferman/Svihra/Aqualina. Chapters on Hays, McCauley, Hancock, Hayes, White, Paul, Adams, Silverman, Edwards, Hicks. Ill. 1941-3 $9.95 p.

CINDERFELLA AND THE SLAM DUNK CONTEST. Elizabeth Burton. An elementary school teacher, together with her 2nd grade class, Elizabeth recreated a Cinderella story around Michael Jordan. Illustrated with 14 color plates by Lynn Offerdahl. ISBN 0-8283-1966-9 $13.95 p.

FREEDOM BY THE BAY--*The Boston Freedom Trail*. William Schofield. The founder of the Boston's Freedom Trail, the author recounts the history of those important and historical events. Ill. 1922-7 $11.95 p.

JACK JOHNSON. Sal Fradella. A pictorial biography of the world's first black heavyweight champion of the world. Illustrated. 1931-6 $9.95 p.

MAKING WISE CHOICES--*A Guide for Women*. C. E. Thompson, M.D. Contains a series of essays on crucial issues confronting modern women--married or single, especially those who may have to make it alone. 1972-3 $12.95 p.

PARKINSON'S--A Personal Story of Acceptance. Sandi Gordon. Autobiography of Sandi as a patient suffering from this dreadful and common disease. Ill. 1949-9 $12.95 p.

PUMPKIN--A Young Woman's Struggle with Lupus. Patricia Fagan. Patricia, the mother of *Pumpkin*, is a professional nurse who more than just looked after her daughter. 1961-8 $12.95 p.

QUIET HERO, THE--A Baseball Story. Rosemary Lonborg, illustrated by Diane Houghton; tells the story of two young boys living with *Gentleman Jim* Lonborg, their father and famous pitcher for the Boston Red Sox. 1958-8 $7.95 p.

SINGLE SOLUTIONS--Essential Guide for the Single Career Woman. Charlotte E. Thompson, M.D. It gives information especially aimed at the single professional woman. 1933-2 $11.95 p.

SONG OF COURAGE, SONG OF FREEDOM. Marilyn Seguin. Tells the story of the child, Mary Campbell, held captive in Ohio by the Delaware Indians from 1759 to 1764. Illustrated. 1952-9 $12.95 p.

Shipping & Handling: *In U.S., $3 first book.*
Master or Visa card orders only: 1-800-359-7031